Ex Domestica

Poems

E.G. Cunningham

C&R Press
Conscious & Responsible

All Rights Reserved

Printed in the United States of America

First Edition
1 2 3 4 5 6 7 8 9

Selections of up to two pages may be reproduced without permissions. To reproduce more than two pages of any one portion of this book write to C&R Press publishers John Gosslee and Andrew Sullivan.

Cover Art by Eugenia Loli
Cover Design by C&R Press

Copyright ©2017 by Elizabeth G. Cunningham

Library of Congress Cataloging-in-Publication Data

ISBN: 978-1-936196-81-4
LCCN: 2017943780

C&R Press
Conscious & Responsible
www.crpress.org

For special discounted bulk purchases please contact:
C&R Press sales@crpress.org

Henry James MacKechnie (1951-2008)

&

Judith Ortíz Cofer (1952-2016)

[I throw the apple at you, and if you are willing to love me, take it and share your girlhood with me; but if your thoughts are what I pray they are not, even then take it, and consider how short-lived is beauty.]

    Plato, *Epigram VII*

[unlove's the heavenless hell and homeless home...lovers alone wear sunlight]

    e.e. Cummings

[I have long had this premonition
Of a bright day and a deserted house.]

    Anna Akhmatova, "Requiem"

Ex Domestica

1.

Breadwinners

       Risking future, I let sugar in. A set of molecules
that used to signal *neighbor*. No window or rap,
no recipe for sharing later.

We go lonely to maintain moral standards,
so we hum anyway, in a decade too late
for landscape. The first imperative:
someone to come home to.

       We modified accordingly. Sets of objects
arranged just so, as if the blade, facing the tine,
might whisper here's how.

The not-said screamed over the living room,
another missed sunset. *First* meaning too long
to count, in a town where time existed
as precipice, though we'd protest not our fault—

and start back.

No glimpse beyond the domestic cage,
where once the erotic apple halved
internal bells. For spite we split
equally, and feigned no count,

invoking the dirty word family
as last resort.

Nightlight

We sought the way back. Searched hard.
We picked along familiar maps, methodical
as highway markers. We thought general,
then thought specific. We began to question
the past, to wonder whether this was always
how it was. We looked up the word apocalypse.

Now and then the view was pleasant enough.
At a certain hour nature mirrored our denouement.
We paused, the sun yolking this to that.
The hour passed.

The loss was gradual, then precipitous.
Familiar maps went missing in the dark.
We laid waste to the receiving halls.
To process the news, we broadcasted it,
we put it to use. What now, we asked.

Tough Love

The open-handed blow—the togetherness
truant—the pocketed rip-off. Mortar estranged
from the brick but I still have my spare key,
still know the ess-curve in the dark by the lake
like the cue to rush toward dinner

but I falter. Something different in the chest
and throat over highbacks and china—
a certain welling up, inappropriate, apropos
of the only holy glint from frosted glass,
means its genitive, on account of,

in the sweat over bread. The pictures come
out: album, from *albus*, that is, some sort
of blanching reaches its bullet to family
en masse. We look on at the past. Sufferers
reattempt.

Change Ringing

How much easier it was—fourteen or so,
burning, confused, a kid—rising and falling
with the *Kyrie, eléison*. With the *caelum et terram*.

To hang from some unseen governor, even
in pain. How safety cloaks into a place of mind.

I've lost that luxury. There are no altars
to usher mayday back to fair. Had I known
this split, this pitting to witness would cost

her light, her changing number—
I might have staved the boom from the wake.

She was a train that I stood by, a halved bell.
I was a spall. The closest star must have shone
then, must now.

Bedside Pulpit

It's not enough to give blood:
to hold a name requires near
transfusion.

Some animal want remembering
me to younger. Mother said
you'll be tired if you close your eyes.

Mercy

There she is, glass mid-air, mauve painting her
poolside face, and she calls that happy.

Me beside her, braid dripping chlorinated water,
my feet burned from the tiled deck.

My father must have taken the picture:
not in the frame, not exactly.

I'm here to entertain, my mother said,
and the statement had

the intended effect—awed laughter.

Men would step through busy streets
back then to offer favors.

I remember at eight years old thinking
don't encourage her.

My hands wasped that day from some flower:
slow, I fisted over the bloom,

and paid for it. Another Polaroid
shows her at a roll-top, hands folded,

nails rose-colored, face whittled,
eyes planetary and frightened.

Through her dress I recognize the cues
of scapulae, elbows. She grins stale through orbit,

she calls that working. As I hold that picture
I remember another, my uncanny settling

into recognition: it's her, not me, not true,
defiance is the bridge between us, past

pink dressing, the photos the same
expression, daring the lens.

Her anger the same root
that makes me turn my head,

and what a way to define ourselves:
the message being, despite prim frosting,

really just a baring of teeth.

Sixteen : The First Dirt

I thought : I was nearly corpsed.
But not yet. Then I felt for a time,
some mark of ontological fade.
        Inhale steam. Exhale plume.

Tarmucking my only chamber
to furnace object relations.

        As if *that* could work. Night swaled
indigo and dark, which wasn't redundant—
Dad had forgotten to change the bulb.

        The house silent then, the walls scratching
the former tenant's epilepsy into me,
threatening—she was a daughter, too,
in the very same room. I flicked
        ash from the open window,
burned to diminish as second best
        to wrench.

The Bright Day

In a car, radio on, landscape
suspension. She's laughing,
so I'm happy, free hand trailing
atmosphere, counting trees,
swaths, clearings. We ill-adapt.

Warm boils over the country
and sieves the highway. It's
morning. I'm eight, nine.
This is summer but only
in mind.

Lone Horse Running

is what I should have said to the silent room that threatened to faint—
projector on, & the crystalline reader yelling to the back of the crowd

adulatory, incanting. Like any good knight I tell the necessary amount
& keep going. Or have you pitched into too & no way to know

who's safe. I unlearn a family retelling. There's the ritual—good—
& the nightmare, locked in. What thrives on repetition. The image

that came was of a single horse running, far afield of
any help or totem—not wounded, no pretty symbol,

just suddenly, in minor shadings, *less there*.
If this were paint it'd be asymptotic, red.

Then my legs, my hands went numb. I felt the familiar electric warning
of the near-unconscious, & shifted my weight, & pretended

into a shuttering off, a single long exposure, of one face, or none.
All eyes swiveled left & right along the walls. The fall lasted five,

ten minutes, imagined. The room, the rows of listeners, at attention.
The speaker: still intoning. Something's wrong with me, I thought—

unsupported transit. A handicap reveals the gaps in locomotion.

& I pictured the lone shot from Muybridge's gun, the bullet
arcing from 1860 to 1874, from the upturned stagecoach

to the mayor's skull. By reason of insanity, sometimes forgiveness:
superimposition obscuring who's safe to tell—how to move through

one point to another in trust of some unifying film. We stood, clapped.
We filed out. A not unsuccessful landing, considering the minutes

before, airborne at the trot, doubting the way back to ground.

Fainter Sets

Maybe blonde listens, but blonde's no antelope.
From the daybed: a view of the church.
And the Sunday hands: in gloves.

From the daybed: wine while we curl
to listen, to reveal the studs—

how that descriptor, *blonde*, meant innocence
before bust, pledge, ménage—
before that autumn's corn color

held us in its faceless pause.

Outside the sidewalks fall to dust
from an earlier world. New frame:
blonde in the doorway. This is impossible

and easy—her hands pale on the couchback,
restless. We listen to chambers meant for

someone else, singing god and miming the chords:
major, minor, fifth, third.

Gentle

There's a way out of this.
Family conversations on car trips.
Slunk far into the leather folds
to keep from inhaling the second-
hand. Even for just thirty minutes.
We were strapped up like cellophane.
I mean we were children.
I never knew we could become
some vogue, some tabled remainder.
I'm still in the car, after all, trees
rush in thick blurs beyond the windows,
your hair reflecting the dinnertime sun: saffron.

A House and a Yard

I have to stop.
I'm running into dust.

It's not a flash,
it's a concertina.

To say car, to say Florida winter,
and my silencer on. And my neurons.
To want to keep the well
without the spilling over.

Why do they describe it as flooding
and maybe when said as missing—

I thought the longer it went on
the provisional would be easier
but in fact…

I used to close my eyes for hours.
And what came of that was—

Minor Preparations

All there anyway. Melody forward:
a figurine adapting, music fleshing
the real girl. Melody back: ex domestica.
I am mother and mother's little helper.

Who thought by this time I would have—
and didn't we all. From the yard: no view,
To get back I'd lie dead on wicker for hours.
To get back I'd give a fist through it,
someone lighting an after-dinner cigar

while I choked happily, a teenage protractor,
not knowing the way I felt about the place
was a kind of in love.

Just-World Hypothesis

We've gone over this. Do
the shoes make the difference,
does the outfit. The carriage,
the hour of appearance.
The answer, repeatedly shed,
is yes. The unsolicited feedback
begs : *Why bring it up again.*
Why not bury the past.

I can't count on one hand—
& those are just the friends.
No room given for the flinch—
no cue to hold back. I can think
of several words that fail
that test of *unto others.*

When X switches M.D.s,
the report goes missing, but "he
felt me up" still rings in my head.
When J pleads with the internet
to "wake up" I think : "it's lost."
The quotient works to subdue
& not much else. A battery
of questions wears the irony
of its own twinning. Our "task,"
once twofold—to grin & bear it—
now pared to the latter.

Hot Property

The escape, a maudlin term,
is counterphobic. Is darts
on nickel beer night in
Temple Terrace. Near one
a.m. is a forearm extension
that makes the rest of the scene

split apart. Is six years later
when I've come to hate the song.
Was the song. Later the host
put on a record, and watched
the pirouette of the brunette
and the famed Lithuanian.
Can you imagine, he said.

Ladies in Wait

To go crazy alone: the unsung
fold. These hills thrum
in sun only. She stays inside.
What difference does it make?
Venetians, or basins, or the varnished
box weathered from an earlier father's
reign. The Deep South's dumb-sharp.
And modern lieutenants' women have no access
to cliffs or chains. After parties what weapons
to flay old celluloid, not to think
of bay or brine—the root remains.

Marrow

1.

Into embers, unencumbered you pass through your own shadow:
a ghost in the molecular crux of an emptying room

the walls and floors moving *just so* in near summer-splinter
in the wake of action almost took. But for the overlay of images

as something other you'd be lost. Should death mean reinvention merely,
merely: were the word to be understood as in the beginning, that is: entirely,

and nothing more. And nothing is: to say truthfully
I less-cloven and at a calm in wait for your re-chiming

where rivers drop to coastal plains, snailing remnants in later hours
and I shell, offerings to cover for your absence

in the flux and wash of it, in the bare-armed neon
the coastal road is mine at six o'clock.

2.

That all my life I've been disconnected from this body: imago:
a ghost who sees ghosts. Half in the doorway –

lost without distinction, and now I sense
that stenciled trope of damage nearly done.

In the blood-strands of our geographical proofs
is the faint echo lub-dub of sea wash

the scaled walls, taupe dunes and old ropes
almond now into some mirage evenly

if *even* intends to signify the same space, tonally:
fully, namely. The circular seals of back-eaten *vacanzas* christening

us informally: some kind of foster-brother or, to slough through extension
relate now-and-then to evening, *sol*-ginger and swooping minutely,

to sensate into that late-early hour, soft particularized panic
in your fingers, in the automobile's fading hum of silenced machinery.

3.

A kidnapping could mean anything: autonomy arrested
on broad avenues by the mind's own volley—in sleep :

intransigence of desire. Rotary. Sidereal movement. In sun,
blinds cut ambient shadows iridescent and pored,

light makes reluctant suspire in morning. And you're standing.

At a low portal retired, the moment pristine, suspended:
hands pull to other centers: I remember, years earlier

the memory too soon, opaque, gelatinous—

Your absence gallops some pain spectacular,
toward the bluing photographs of afternoon.

4.

And dear Henry:

no traffic, no turret, no red brick. Long exposure of lux seconds
of cleft and worked-over sidewalk. Plum lizards.

Silent cemeteries. Thought nebulous and arterial both:
shower through cumulus: brief and intermittent like commas

And dear Henry:

the soft-dead oscillation of indoor synoptics.
The circuitous ping and reverb of the feint

and double barreled and stuccoed shotgun,
The hearse in park at the parlor across the street.

beyond that, beyond the hold and toss
of the *quercus* and *lache* in which I "grew up"

And dear Henry:

at a time when getting through the music
as best as possible was the standard, sometimes

a single flute broke standard complement
a ragged shoot from the footpath concrete, a crescendo

or uncurrying. The impatiens convective, bundled
or simply: thinking of you.

And dear Henry:

there is today and there is today and where you are
lined apricot and macrocosmic will not rust, but cycle seasons.

That we both cherried answers from strands' blooming vistas:
a blunting art where oceans were higher,

when worked by apparition.

Florida Desperate

You always were my exit 329.

I too had a gold ring.
I had other soundtracks, once.
Flowers. Followers. I'm not
joking. I'm charming it up.

The days sweat through the car
you laughed like a machine gun
there were exceptions.

Taken in a blur I've felt
happy this whole time.
The days cheer like a march.
I get the symphonies mixed up.

I'll do this last and come to love
these rooms' smallnesses

come to get me before it closes
on something definitive.

2.

Cameos

To revisit is a kind of danger.
Like the summer burned in a barn
over Beaujolais and secrets—
four women terrified of the not-yet-
to-come, coming undone.

Doll's secret was a double death,
a painting by someone else. Blue's
was sitting next to her, in a wrap skirt
and drunk. Mine was blue,

though I didn't know it yet—
I had two then—one bud waiting,
the other over-bloomed, the need
to hazard, and again hazard, despite
the scar.

The night dimmed on. A sound
at the door like the tide
pulling under.

One by one, the landscape cut
from us. I think of them: Doll north,
blue's love a Hollywood front, blue
still blue but as an ozone fading, me
twinning our wakes, bruising our negatives.

Amour-propre

That wasn't the plan—not even close.
When we go south I cease thinking
in pictures and trip words. Four lines,

or: our first initials, cardinal points
in a dissolving country. Closer
would be affected by silence, hurt.

Memory seals the haircut you gave
yourself, an inscription in a thin book.
The path stuck for years like a road
to Oz, the loss still latent, its far-off
thunder once comforting, now
swelled to enclosure.

Banner Sky, Blue Barriers

The gate won't latch.
My first time in a strange house

and now, midnight, leaving,
I struggle with the hinge

of the front yard gate.
A low echo wings

internal, post-avian.
The door swings open.

He's just a recognizeable
face. Across the street, a bulb

hangs flaccid light, reveals
a scrape of road. I stare

at the asphalt, the TV wash.
How have I come to split

myself sparked—how have
I come to raid and be raided.

Why, in that swollen moment,
did I witness
such unnecessary beauty.

A Valuable Piece of Air

You said, map here. I did. What the terrain
whispered I kept. Slower, fast. And forgotten

to a change of season and until then a
Morse politeness. When the waves hit—

made of anything—ground lifts. Blue or
the future whose dreams cartographers

capture: new. Us, we searched for a kind
of money. In the reproduction of euphoria

we felt nothing good. Or if light means
crispest sight, a snowfall.

Rayleigh Scattering

End of the year gray. Anchors
where balloons should be, or
could peace wait on the outer
bank of sane. How in the holiday
buzz to say nothing for clear, that is:
give me back remembering.
Its attendant costumed sting.
The portraiture made overkill
by rain. No incoming. The quantum
state the same. The slide the black,
the self-quilled quell to love
the heartburn sun, its citrus sky.
If only.

Self-Portrait as a Series of Near Misses

Lapses in chains prevented
certain tragedies. Like night
runner, under streetlamps,
handled, not quite attacked.

Some shout into stone
turning my head. In water,
fished out by a pair of hands.

Or recompensed: karmic buzz
candystriping my almost arrival,
a thank-god striking against
a tonal third, the chord also pinging

it can't be and why this. The car intact.

The blood clotted, beaten back.
The hand recovering materials
again. Sometimes caught breath
edged relief, awed at the minor slip,
kneeled to humble or cursed the damage.

Animal Rituals

So what if skin goes stinging
and raw over breakfast. Meaning weeping
we maraud into yoghurt. The ersatz
creamer oily and gulf in the reddest
mug. And blackberries, their pebbled
domes, their drupes I love. Crows
fade into wings. The stage is
not the stage. Monitors speak back
our needs. Of pretending to have
always seen what just appeared,
to unlearn a honing instinct.

Resentment / Risorgimento

Too much? I can be crueler than that.
Replay the deck. An unlaced Achilles
limping nowhere. And if the body's a temple
something felled too early and if I'm up late
it's a bad sign, regardless of age.

Replay the deck.

A neon glow beyond the underpass.
A woman airbrushed in pretend wind-swept
and within stucco walls *real girls* cool
their tempers for numbers, cash—

it's not that I remember every song.

It wan'ts the chrome, the cinch
that stitched men together—weal / welt
did that. And troops still die in want or waste.

I obeyed sentiment by unlacing.
And paid later with the southern question—
to "feel again," solo in the bourbon wing

sans vespers, and, naked or clothed,
incensed nonetheless. No sailors on deck.
But if you'd gathered us…

The Media Room

What a real boy would.
We've a duty to—
what, exactly?
Performance piety.
Dilettante suffering.
Stacks of facts
tizzy the system.
Temps rise, talk turns
to margins. What a real heart
would, what a trend.
What's a shard,
what's a share
between friends.

Wish Fulfillment

perfume the entire swath
from pith to root—

to rot: some key
you stick to.

a picture of, of course,
the whole shebang.

to squall or squash the cello
in the chest: an unlocked code.

In Situ

The situation: inside me, unclear—
as if I can *feel* the twists,
the mitochondrial fits inches deep
in that place made to toil and holy
both, rooted in and in itself
a serpentine path, an Edenic *pomme*.

I hold the on-site seedling original,
rotting, a post-Biblical body : from sin
to carcinogen, and imagine the adobe cracks,
the histology. A miniature Gobi, a cellular
Atacama, a hollow harm, a *kytospathos*.

To diagnose the nucleus : Russian-nested
in a maybe-future embryo. I sit in the idea
of mass suspension—one growth yolked
to diminish me, the other which might
expand beyond its initial founding.

Ovid

Little mass, big pain, goes the song
of the self. I hum mausoleum to a
stranger's steps. Awaiting the results
isn't different from not, I tell myself.
Gray for weeks. The town shuts its
mouth to dream vacations, utopian
versions of the real. Mine is you
reacting just so, which is different,
what no tonic can withdraw,
unfold. My nondescript hands
never surgeon's. This town stains
of heaving, fuel.

Marriage of Opposites

Tossed the lit match
behind me. Drove out
speeding. Fiction—that's not
even close. What really
happened: a quiet numb
leaving, keys in hand, wishing
for epiphany. Half in the doorway,
half in the spring soundtrack,
cold and too crow for crying.

Noon at the Edge of a Field

Modulation spins bombs into parade.
I pirouette the small cell of pure O.
Now the three miles to work while glass
replays the my god my god, sidelining
pretty vistas, any presence of—not mind—
some kind of stirring. Receded past
panic in a stippled field. Voices weal.
There used to be someplace else:
a self pressed into the world, staunch
and elemental as dirt. Who wouldn't
have known of repair, or cared.

3.

Annus / Versus

If you, in a park / peal spiritual
let me come running—opal streak

& the sky grieves its sun-
oracle foretelling, & the sky

rejoices simply being. If dizzy
like flowers let there be pollen,

at least between my growth &
diminution—with each turning

I long frightfully to know: why
any passage / any sea-change

at all: the penances the costs
stored up inside my history stamp

of guilt. I crawl to cordon off
to refocus on: steep grade. Stream

of the evident love / the animal
underneath. I drown for a swear:

worry the question & quit
the contrary—begging the cycle

to hold me suspended / suspiring
at the ever-cleansing threshold.

Forms of Nature

To be your *malo, mela,* your garden anything—
to mate I fell nondescript as aha clover, name
notwithstanding, scrubbed over. You my prep-,
post-, adposition. You my stranding. At three years
studies claim falsehoods, sentences,
frames of reference, but we've childhooded
backward to a nonblinking stand and tumble.

      The household branches bear no olives—some chemical
lost in transversal from dendrite to axon, or,
put another way, from your eye to mine : some L word
follicle gone bald. To an afternoon when I dressed
purple to please you, the history conjecture
a stretched frame, and, as ever, afternoon,
for after each other's five o'clock,
you always my five o'clock, no matter
what setting comes later.

Channels for Water

Or where does the Raadhuisstraat go
if I recite your name. January,
& I'm soaked in rain a woman
made older by anger, ungoverned—
I walk to pretend purpose, still lost.

No epiphany blooming along the Nine
Canals, or the Rembrandts. Till dusk,
to dial you, you the everyone preempting
departure, each face an amalgam of my
mistakes.

I walk until I can't stand, imagining your consonants
over paperbacks along the Spui—an echo of

a student, who once said : Heathcliff's
a psycho. If I couldn't explain—no Thames,
no Garden of England—the cause was over-

identification. Smoke clears along the quay.
There, two hundred names.

Bad Love Song

There's a way out of this
sketch. A mercurial self,
the self convex, tubal ligation,
atrium blown open, and there it goes.
The same history of over the top.
In dawn the line out is long—
we're fenders on the body asphalt.
And have overstepped those organs
just for a say so, but now that's
resting

Pine

Slide the video in. Lost the flagship.
Poor and empty, I took to materials,
not *seriatim* but matryoshka
nonetheless. In rained
Saturday, the ersatz hull
of the husk close to touch
through music, six o'clock—
any sunset the set point
for late mourning

Aurochs / Inter in May

Periodic & blocked off—not to say pine
or herb of any kind, not to say citrus—

left searching for the apt material, that is
touchable : to improvise your resurrection

means adoption / adaptation—improved responses
to perennial tics—espying a calendar, turning

the cellular handwriting over. Blue—
over the years I've studied you, wishing accrual

as consolation : every detail banded—as if detected
could mean extant—the aha waylaid by dual creation

of clue & case. The P.I. in me pauses to pretend
who I'm trailing. Your domesticated waste. There

are days I urge you to sand, to silt the shingles of
our invisible house, invisible past—you did, after all

exist once. You were, above all, a standing animal—

even if no one can term me your bearing, even alone
& stripped of any unison, any *remember when*—

or fill in the blank. I have pictures : '80s tint, their
cardstock heft a sacrificial window I fall through,

again. To thresh through your Taurus & no
landing to speak of. I pay to make you up.

I pay to sit to hear trained strangers
say: *get over it*. Or :

can you expound on that. Or : *grieving process*—
that route never finite. Like stars. As in : used-to-be.

I don't need help with the fleshing out. If you
knew how many landscapes death laminates.

Maybe you do. I need someone to utter : *he died.*
Is dead. Won't rise. Let it sink in. Still I beat back

the shriek to conserve the beast of you—
stiffen incarnadine & fade into that period

of in-between : spring's coda. Not-yet
summer—to mourn would be to swelter

your preservatives—to play it safe, I park.

ACKNOWLEDGEMENTS

I am grateful to the editors of the following magazines and journals, in which some of these poems first appeared: *em—a review of text and image, Fjords Review, Hobart, La Vague, Locomotive, The Nation, Poetry London, Prick of the Spindle, Propeller Magazine, Quiddity, Rhino, Rust + Moth, SAND*, and *The Volta*.

Thank you to Seth Abramson, Bradley Bazzle, Johnny Damm, Alex Duensing, Will Dunlap, Jay Hopler, Jodi Johnson, Jane Lewty, Karen MacKechnie, John A. Nieves, Daniele Pantano, Ed Pavlić, and Andrew Zawacki. Thank you to Matthew Nye and thank you to my family.

ABOUT THE AUTHOR

E.G. Cunningham is the author of *Apologetics*. She holds an MFA from the Iowa Writers' Workshop and a PhD in Creative Writing from the University of Georgia.

OTHER C&R PRESS TITLES

FICTION

Ivy vs. Dogg
by Brian Leung

A History of the Cat In Nine Chapters or Less
by Anis Shivani

While You Were Gone
by Sybil Baker

Spectrum
by Martin Ott

That Man in Our Lives
by Xu Xi

SHORT FICTION

Meditations on the Mother Tongue
by An Tran

The Protester Has Been Released
by Janet Sarbanes

ESSAY AND CREATIVE NONFICTION

While You Were Gone
by Sybil Baker

Je suis l'autre: Essays and Interrogations
by Kristina Marie Darling

Death of Art
by Chris Campanioni

POETRY

Negro Side of the Moon
by Early Braggs

Holdfast
by Christian Anton Gerard

Ex Domestica
by E.G. Cunningham

Collected Lies and Love Poems
by John Reed

Imagine Not Drowning
by Kelli Allen

Les Fauves
by Barbara Crooker

Tall as You are Tall Between Them
by Annie Christain

The Couple Who Fell to Earth
by Michelle Bitting

CHAPBOOKS

Cuntstruck by Kate Northrop

Relief Map by Erin Bertram

Love Undefined by Jonathan Katz

www.ingramcontent.com/pod-product-compliance
Lightning Source LLC
Chambersburg PA
CBHW022001100426
42738CB00042B/1302